What Am I?

WRITTEN, DESIGNED and ILLUSTRATED by LENN REDMAN

ISBN: 978-0-9606258-4-0
Published by Mark Victor Publishing, Co.,
a division of Redman Artworks, LLC.
www.redmanartworks.com

INTRODUCTION

Many great people over the years have raised their voice against prejudice. Like Abraham Lincoln and his famous statement, 'All men are created equal', most have emphasized our similarities. But artist Lenn Redman believed this premise could never succeed in overcoming prejudice. "There is no prejudicial Caucasian who could possibly be convinced that he is anything like his Black, Hispanic or Oriental contemporaries. The converse is equally true. The fact is nothing in existence is exactly like its counterparts. People are as different from each other as leaves on a tree and that's fine, its nature's design!"

Redman believed the most effective way to thwart national and ethnic prejudice is by educating people to this reality: mankind's composition of a multitudinous variety is what we have, not in opposition to, but in common with each other. Our differences are supplementary and can be used beneficially for universal needs.

For those unfamiliar with poetic abstractions, you'll have no trouble understanding Redman's motive to offset racial and national prejudice and its implications.

- *What Am I = What Are We*
- *No two people are exactly alike*
- *We keep changing in our appearance and in our thinking*
- *We should be tolerant of each other*
- *We can use our differences for each other's good*

Thank you for supporting our mission to bring humanity together despite our differences. Lenn's legacy lives on through his work, his family, and his mission. Please, join us at redmanfamilyfoundation.org and help us make a difference.

MARK VICTOR PUBLISHING CO.

What Am I?

I am People, that's what I AM.

I am man, woman, child and infant.

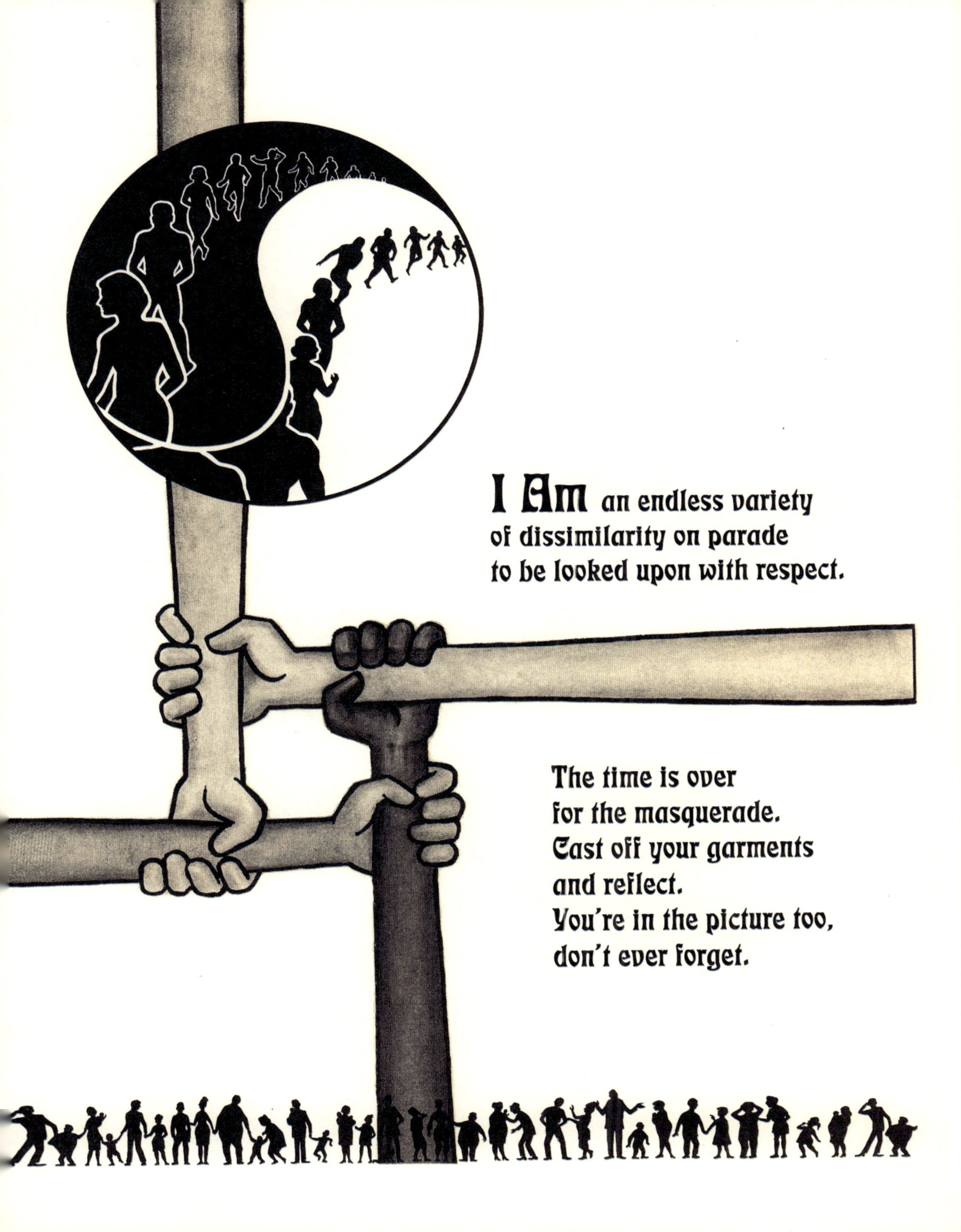
I Am an endless variety
of dissimilarity on parade
to be looked upon with respect.

The time is over
for the masquerade.
Cast off your garments
and reflect.
You're in the picture too,
don't ever forget.

What A Face I have!

It varies in size, texture, shape and slope,
like that of a cactus, gourd and cantaloupe.

My Eyes, Nose, Mouth and Ears

are large, small, long, short, flat, bulbous, narrow and wide.
And the spaces between my features
are as varied as the features themselves.

It Has Been Said

they show my soul, those organs called eyes
which bulge, recede, droop, squint, glare and dart,
and are round, narrow, slanty, close together and far apart.

Of course they show my soul, my eyes,
but no more so than the top of my head
or the orbs in my skies.

And I Am Multicolored.

I am a peculiar hue of red, yellow, white, black,
brown, tan, gray, pink, bronze, copper, gold
and a thousand shades of each.
I am as united by the spectrum of my different colors
as the planets are united by their orbital relationships.

What if?

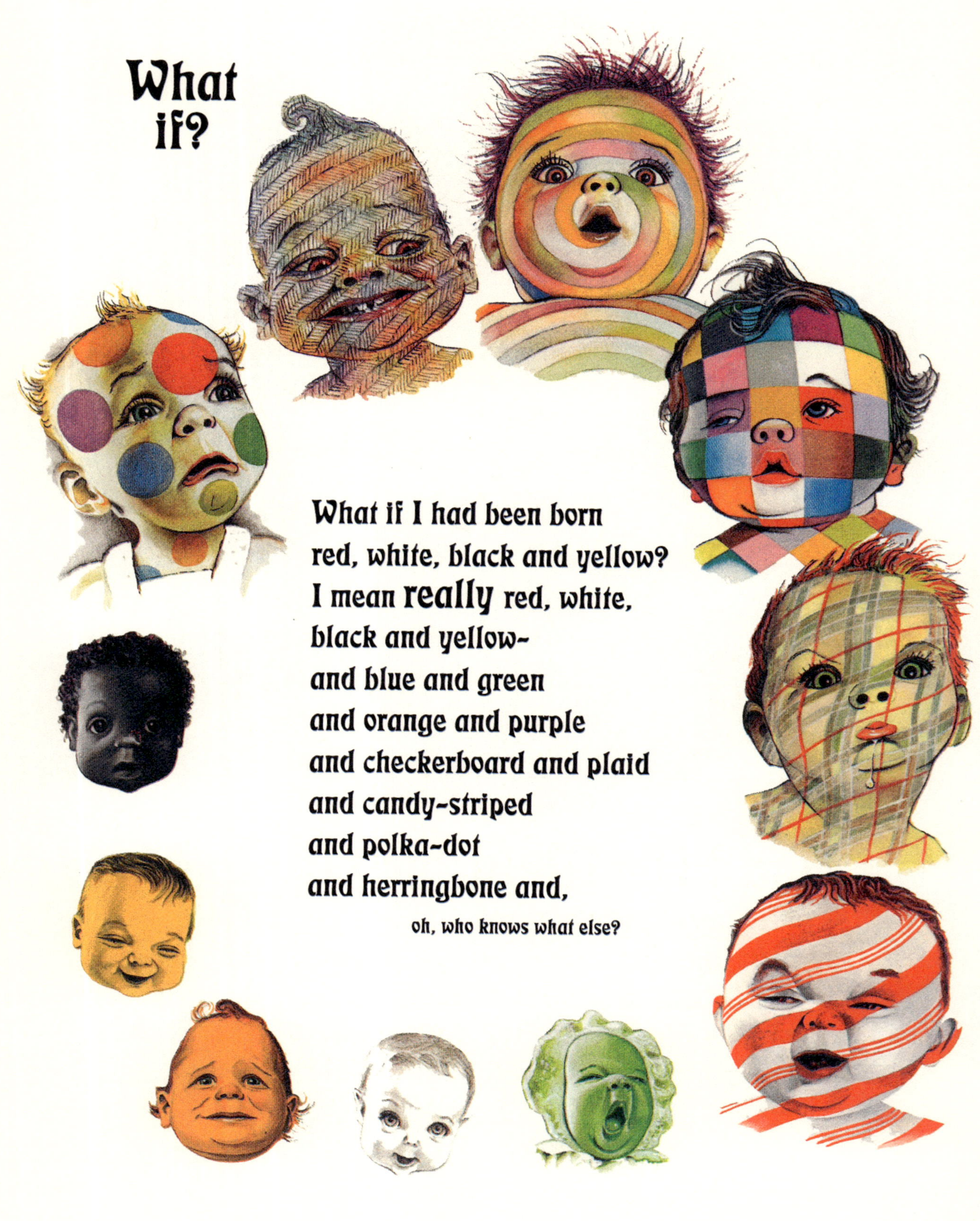

What if I had been born
red, white, black and yellow?
I mean **really** red, white,
black and yellow–
and blue and green
and orange and purple
and checkerboard and plaid
and candy-striped
and polka-dot
and herringbone and,

oh, who knows what else?

I Am What I Am!

And I must **KNOW** what I am,
for some day I will see myself
from other planets~

And who knows what I will see?

I Will See

there are more differences.
to my makeup
than I've ever imagined.
Is there the slightest possibility
I'd accept myself with objectivity,
if not good will and mirth,

before I've purged myself
of all hostility
to what there is of me
right here on earth?

What Am I?

I am a symbiotic temple
of seeming contradictions, partial understanding
of which may be had by asking questions.
Once the answers are known, man will begin to tower.
Is there a similarity between the bee
and the flower?

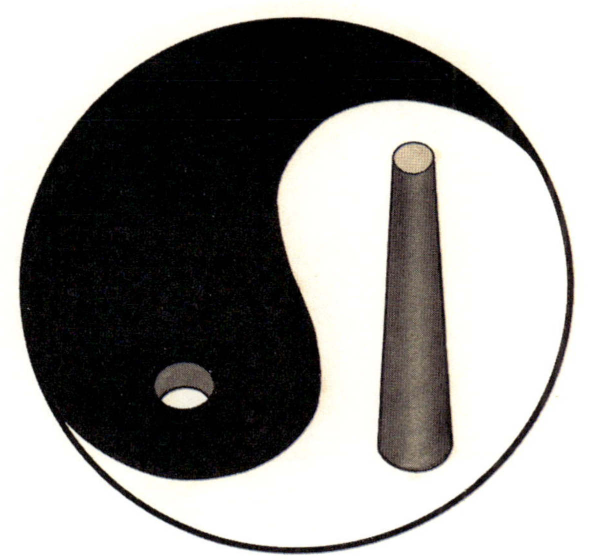

Is black any more different from white
than white is different from black?

Is a peg any more different from a hole
than a hole is different from a peg?

And what of the circle, square and triangle,
the three most oposite geometric forms?

Is one more different from the others
than the others are different from the one?

The Answers, of course are no; and that is their commonality. The flower and the bee are not at all alike, yet they thrive on each other's existence. And black and white make a thousand beautiful shades of gray. And a peg and a hole may effectuate a strong inseparable bond. And the circle, square and triangle constitute the architectural foundation for my temple of universal design.

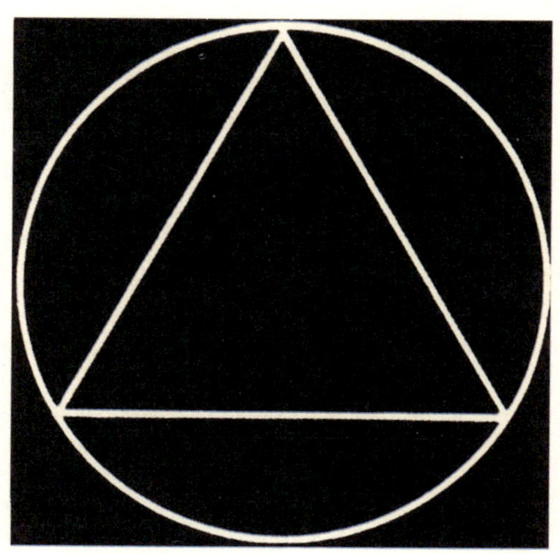

I Am A Rhapsodic Symphony Of Differences

But my differences are not individually more unique than their respective counterparts.

I AM a throbbing, pulsating spirit.
always on the move, always changing,
interplaying with and reacting to
the various components of my whole.
They comprise infinite semblances
that are as varied and different
as night and day.
Yet from Infinity's vantage --
Night And Day Are The Same.

What Am I?
I Am The Glow In Flight.
I Am It
And It Is I,
And You And I and It
Are One.

I AM THAT, I AM.

50th Anniversary Edition

Carrying on the legacy of
Lenn Redman

At the height of Lenn Redman's career, he was animating for huge studios and redefining the world of caricatures as he traveled and performed his art across the country.

Lenn Redman at the 1980 release of "What Am I?"

No amount of success could distract him from the reality of what was going on in his world. With the assassination of President Kennedy and civil rights leader like Martin Luther King, Jr., Lenn decided he had to do more than what he was already doing.

It was at this time that he wrote the poem, "What Am I?" and began fighting for equality and speaking out about the crimes against humans around the world. He spoke passionately and spread his message as far as he could.

Today, his son, Mark Redman, and Mark's family, are continuing the legacy that Lenn started. Through the Redman Family Foundation, Mark is helping to spread the message of inclusion and love to the world while empowering young artists through various scholarship programs and benefits.

The Redman Family Foundation believes that every individual is unique and special, yet we are all the same. The world today is not so different from the world that Lenn saw in his time. We don't want another generation to come and go before that changes. It starts with us, a voice of hope, taking the words and art of a brilliant man who loved deeply and bringing them to life in a world that needs them more now than ever.

Join us on the path to change. Visit www.redmanfamilyfoundation.org to donate or get involved.

In addition to this book, Lenn printed 12 large format pieces of art.
Shown are 6 examples of the prints.

Prints are available at lennredman.com in the following sizes:
8"x10", 12"x16", 18"x24", 24"x36"

Made in the USA
Columbia, SC
31 January 2025